Introduction to "WISH YOU WERE HERE in North Berwick"

Scotland has some wonderful scenery, and not just in the Highlands and Islands. Less than 25 miles east of Edinburgh, on the Firth of Forth, the East Lothian town of North Berwick has its own magic and charm. It is a short direct train or road journey from Edinburgh and is a gem of a place to live, to holiday in and to visit.

This 'big picture' book brings together my favourite local photographs taken throughout the year in and around North Berwick, the "Biarritz of the North".

Enjoy

Ian Goodall

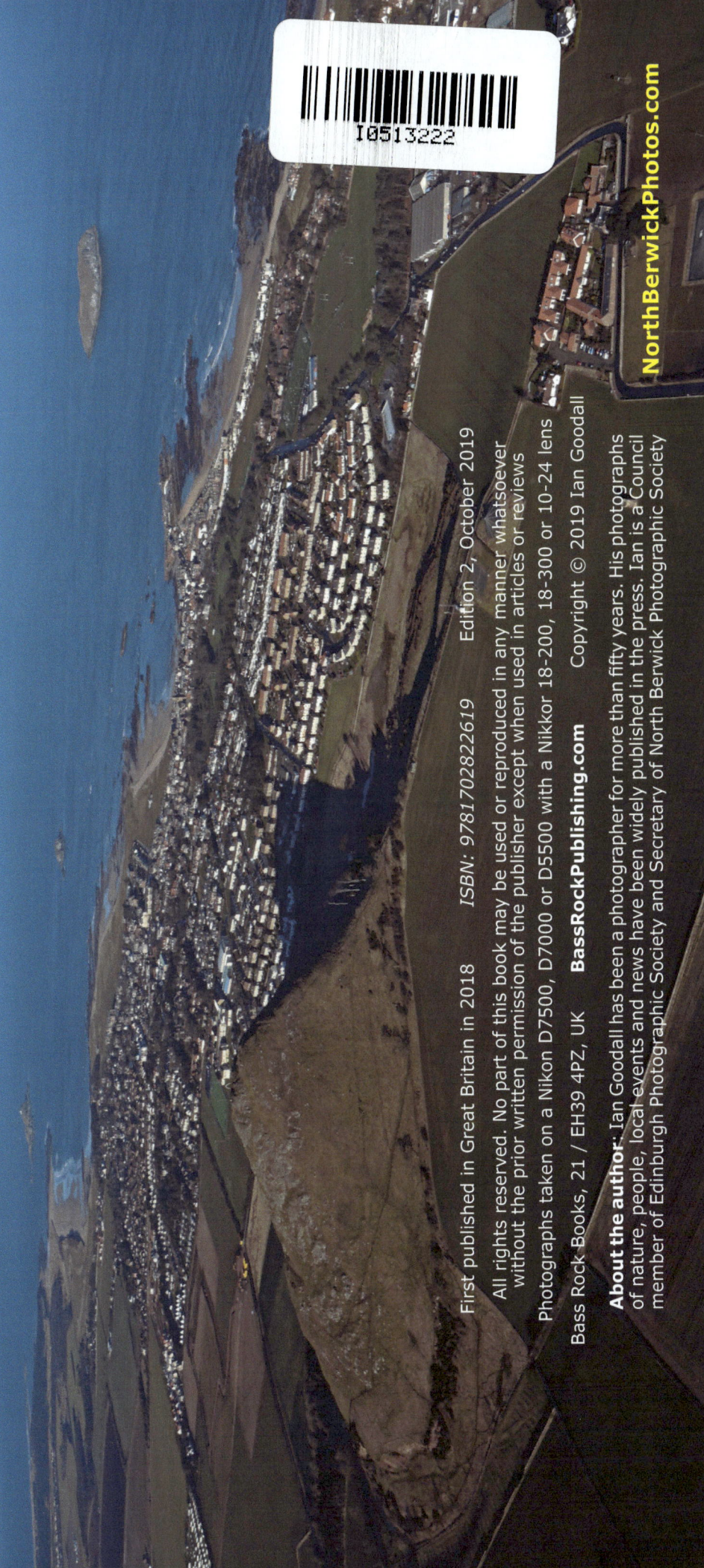

First published in Great Britain in 2018　　ISBN: 9781702822619　　Edition 2, October 2019

All rights reserved. No part of this book may be used or reproduced in any manner whatsoever without the prior written permission of the publisher except when used in articles or reviews

Photographs taken on a Nikon D7500, D7000 or D5500 with a Nikkor 18-200, 18-300 or 10-24 lens

BassRockPublishing.com　　Copyright © 2019 Ian Goodall

Bass Rock Books, 21 / EH39 4PZ, UK

About the author: Ian Goodall has been a photographer for more than fifty years. His photographs of nature, people, local events and news have been widely published in the press. Ian is a Council member of Edinburgh Photographic Society and Secretary of North Berwick Photographic Society

NorthBerwickPhotos.com

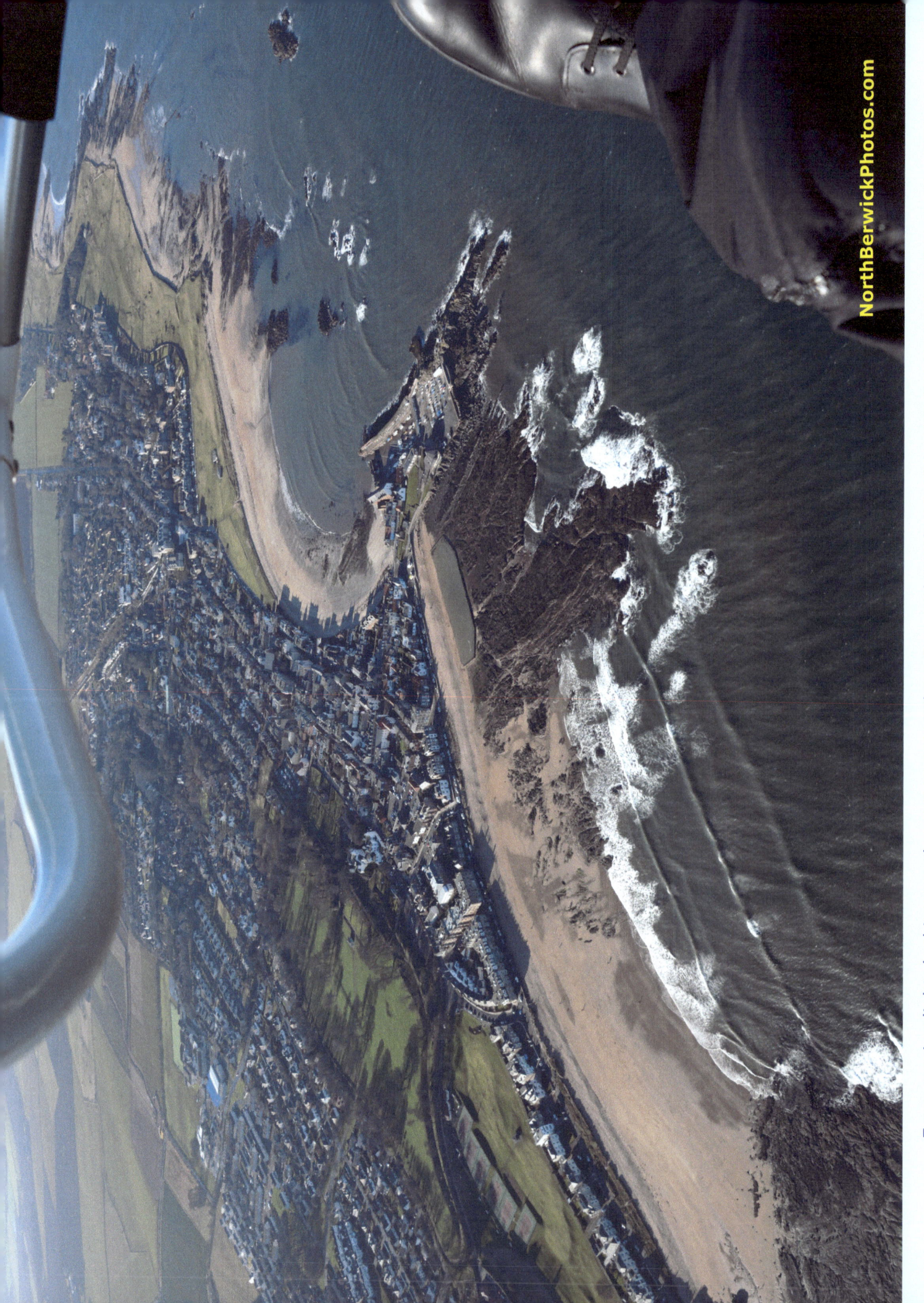

From a microlight, looking south-west across Milsey Bay and North Berwick with the harbour at the centre-right

Looking north across North Berwick. A superimposed model of St Andrew's Auld Kirk shows how it could have looked in the 1600s

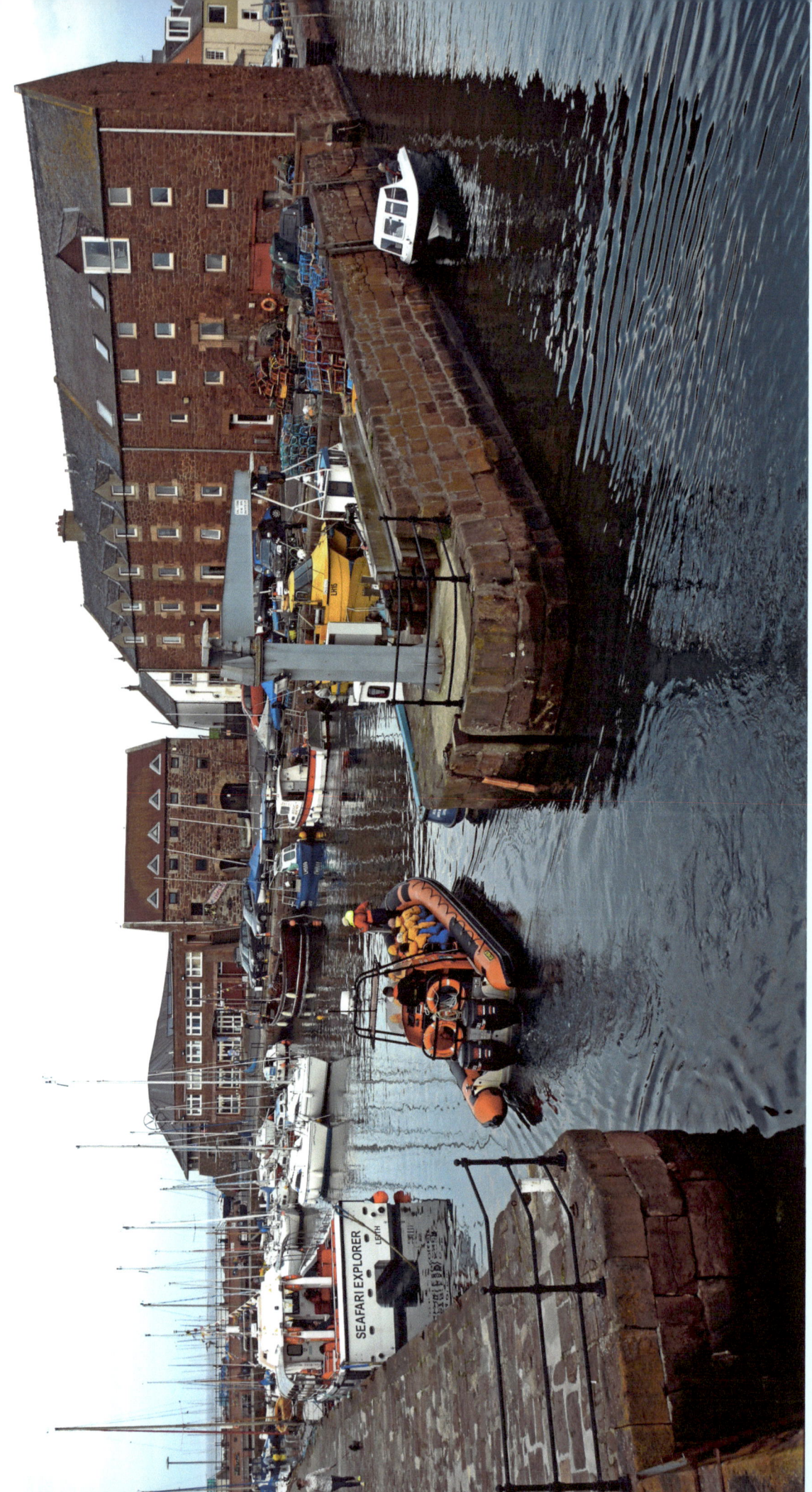

North Berwick harbour. A Seabird Centre boat has just returned from a trip to the Isle of May

North Berwick harbour

NorthBerwickPhotos.com

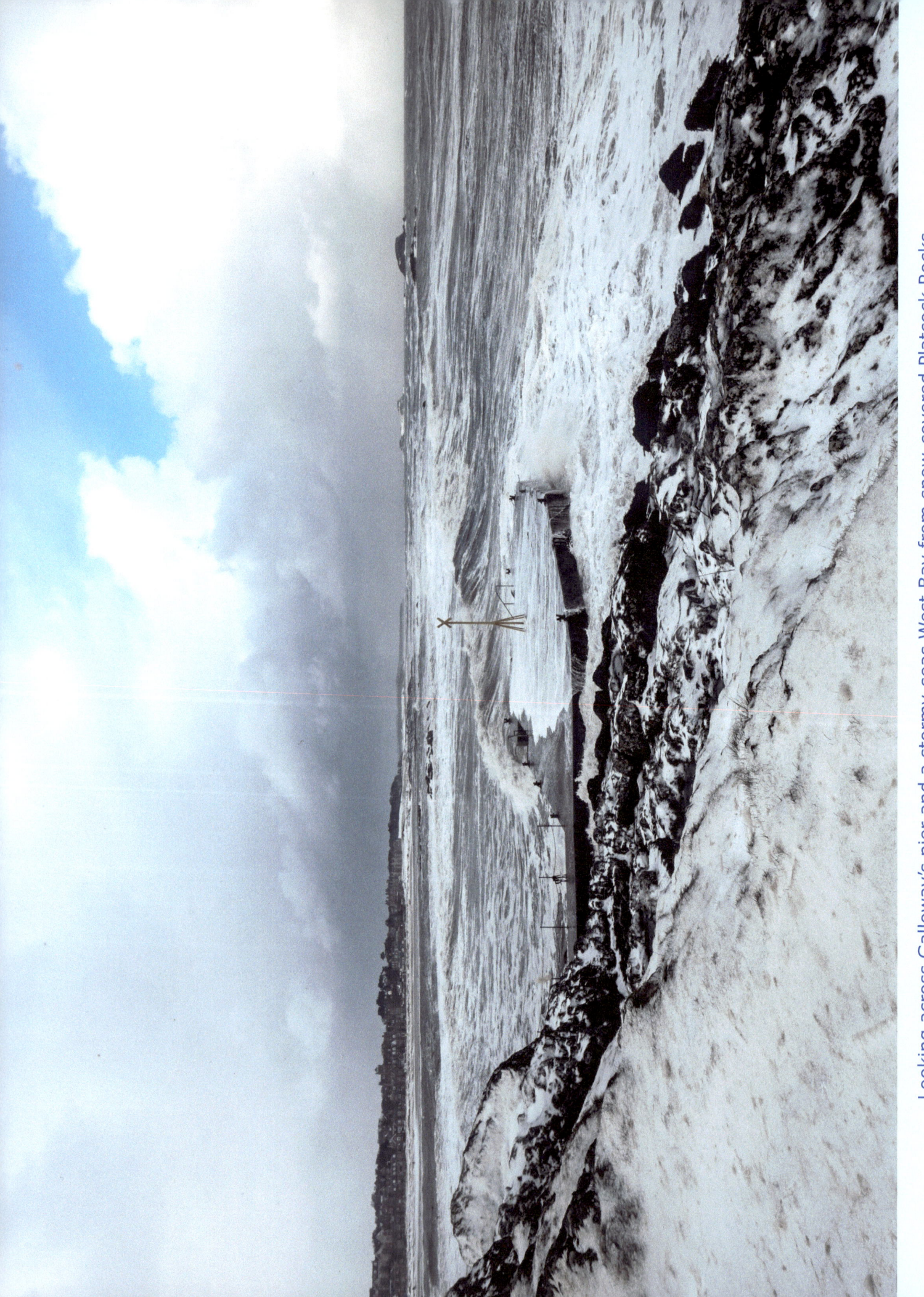

Looking across Galloway's pier and a stormy-seas West Bay from snow-covered Platcock Rocks

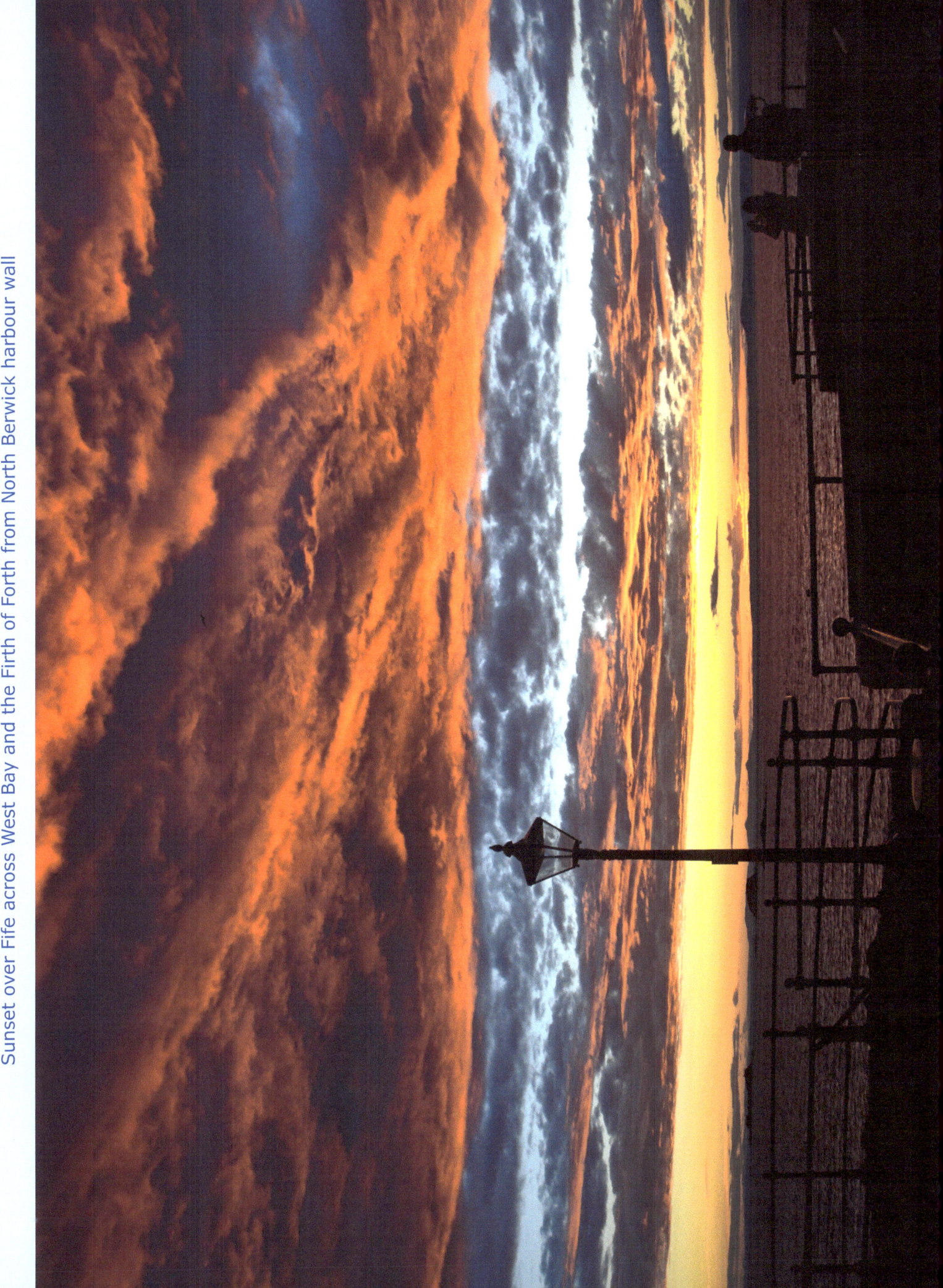
Sunset over Fife across West Bay and the Firth of Forth from North Berwick harbour wall

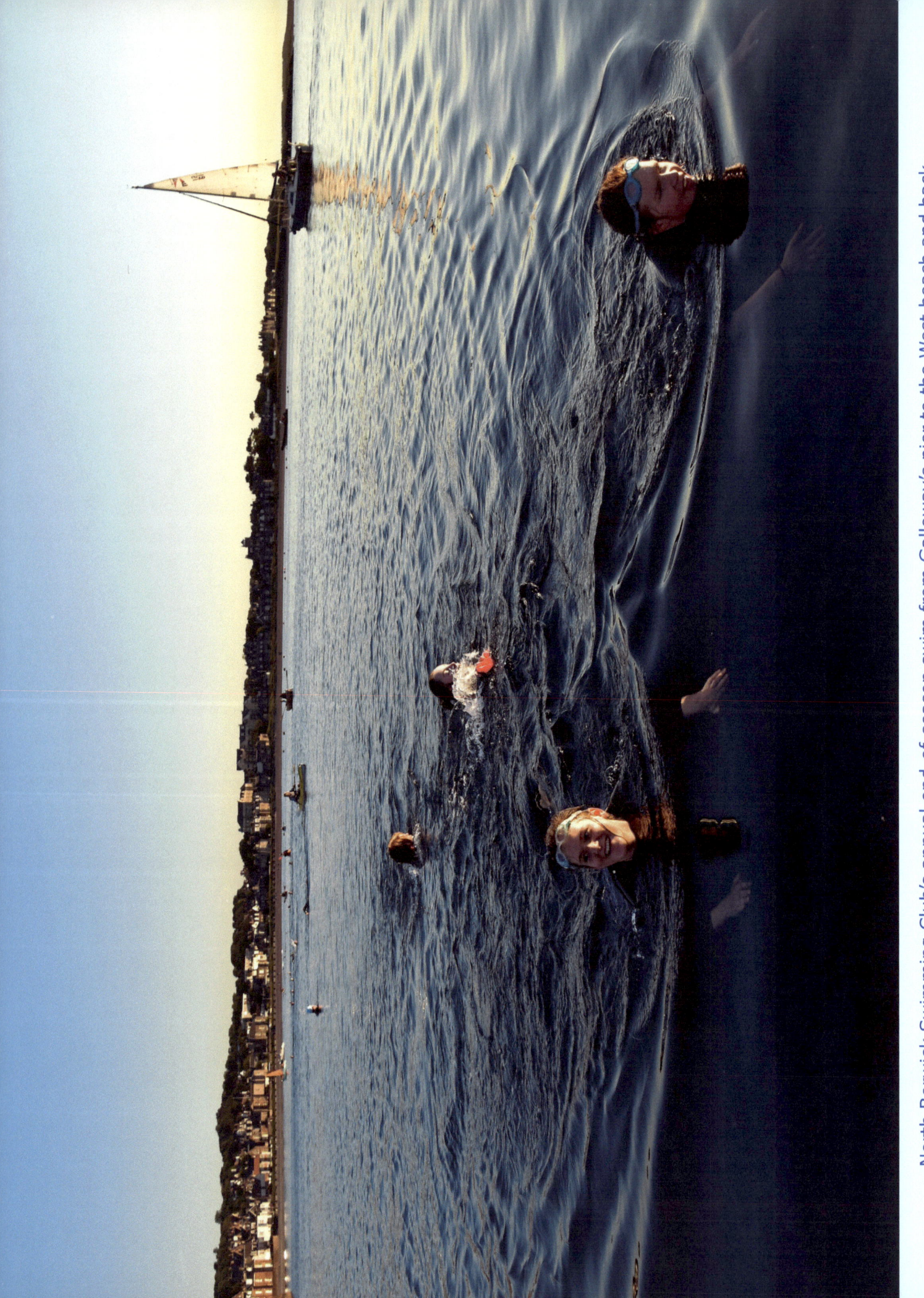

North Berwick Swimming Club's annual end-of-season swim from Galloway's pier to the West beach and back

North Berwick Rowing Club's August regatta when skiffs race out to and round the Craig and back

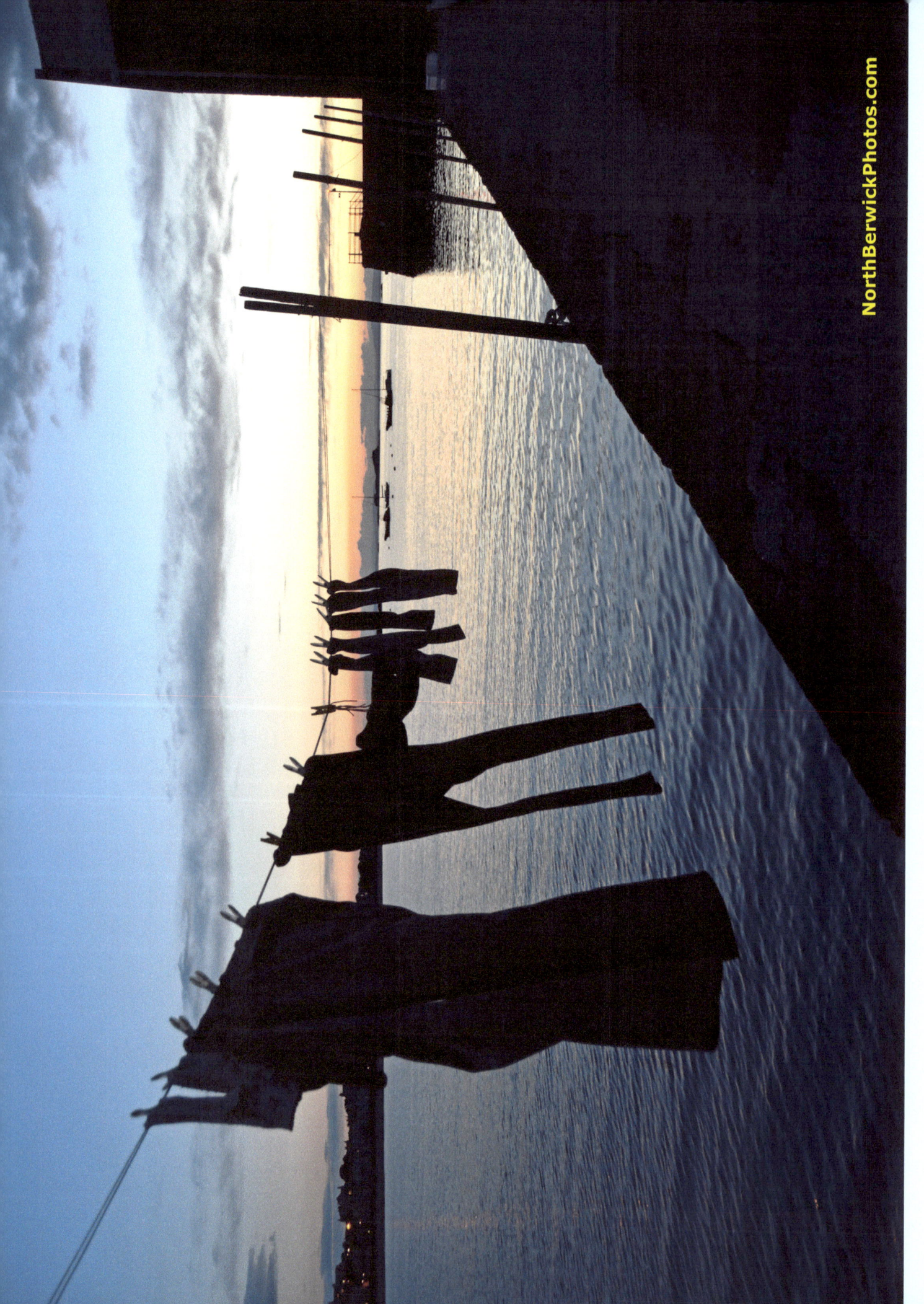

Low Quay washing and sunset over Fife

NorthBerwickPhotos.com

Low Quay washing and East Lothian Yacht Club sailing dinghies

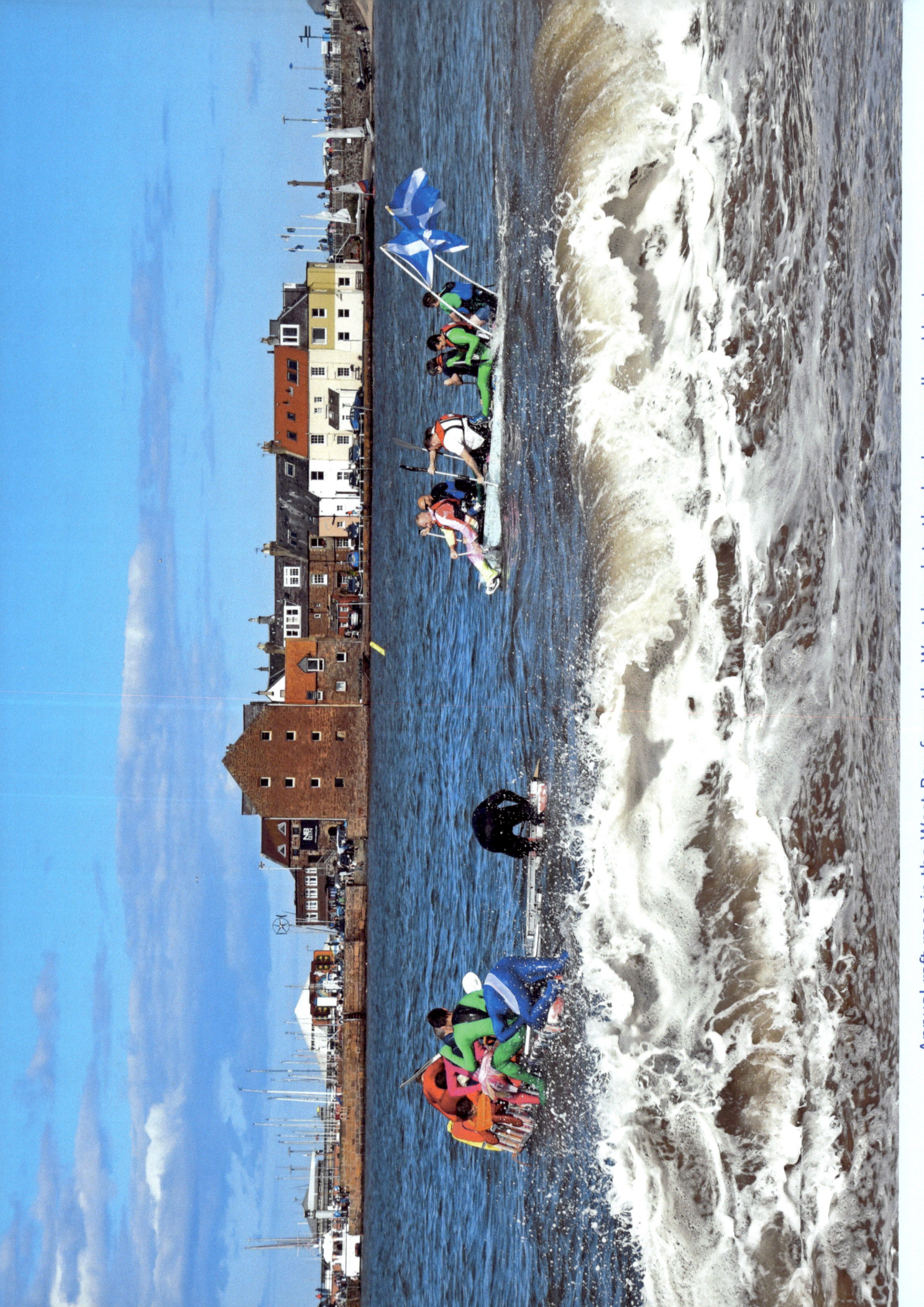

Annual raft race in the West Bay from the West beach to the harbour wall and back

West Bay and beach

West beach sunset

A New Year's Day West Bay rainbow over Craigleith

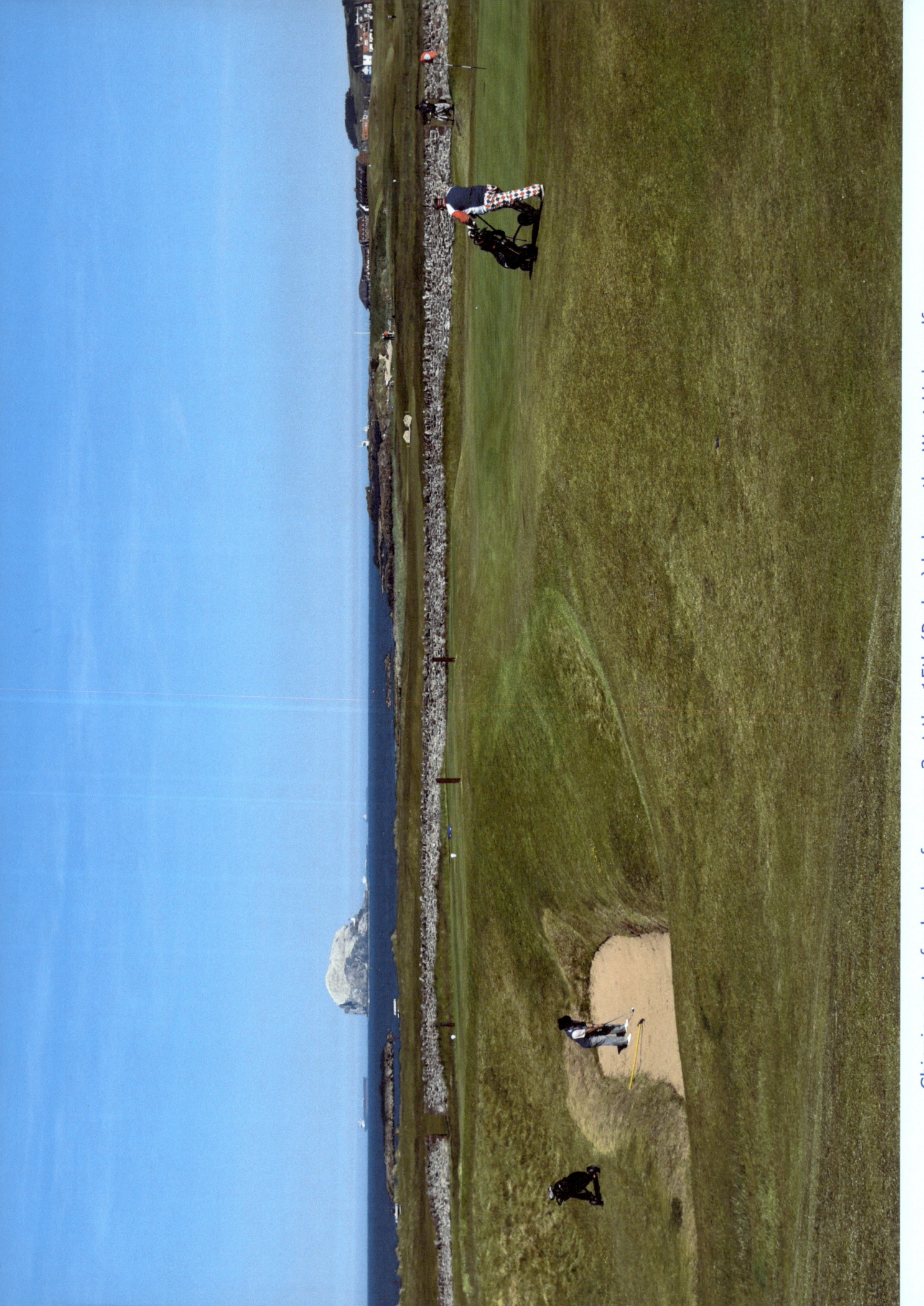

Chipping out of a bunker for a par 3 at the 15th (Redan) hole on the West Links golf course

TOP: North Berwick Rowing Club regatta, West Bay and beach

BOTTOM: West Links golf course, 17th green

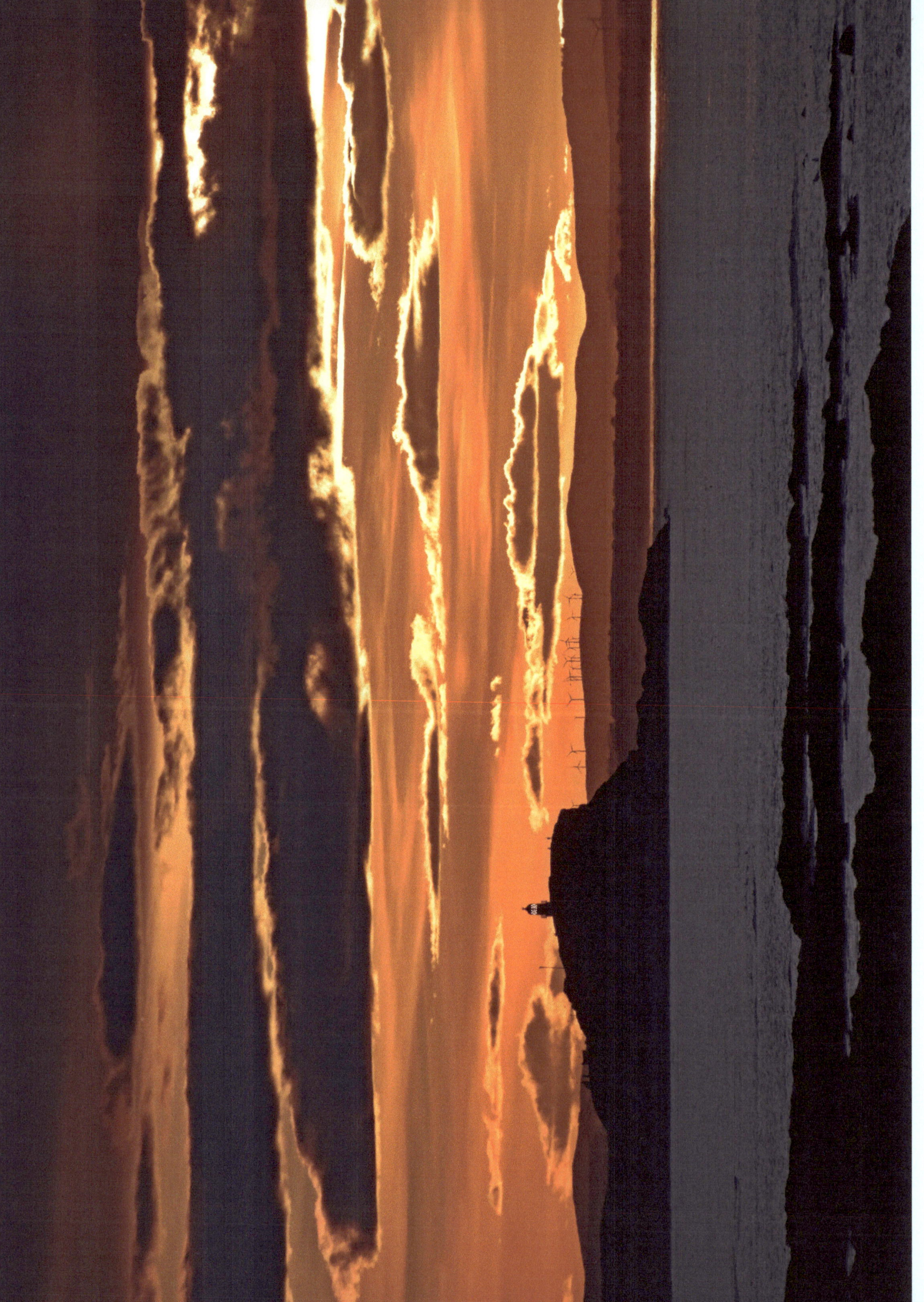
Sunset over Fidra and Fife

Island of Fidra (Robert Louis Stevenson's "Treasure Island") from Yellowcraig beach. The Lomond Hills (Fife) are in the distance

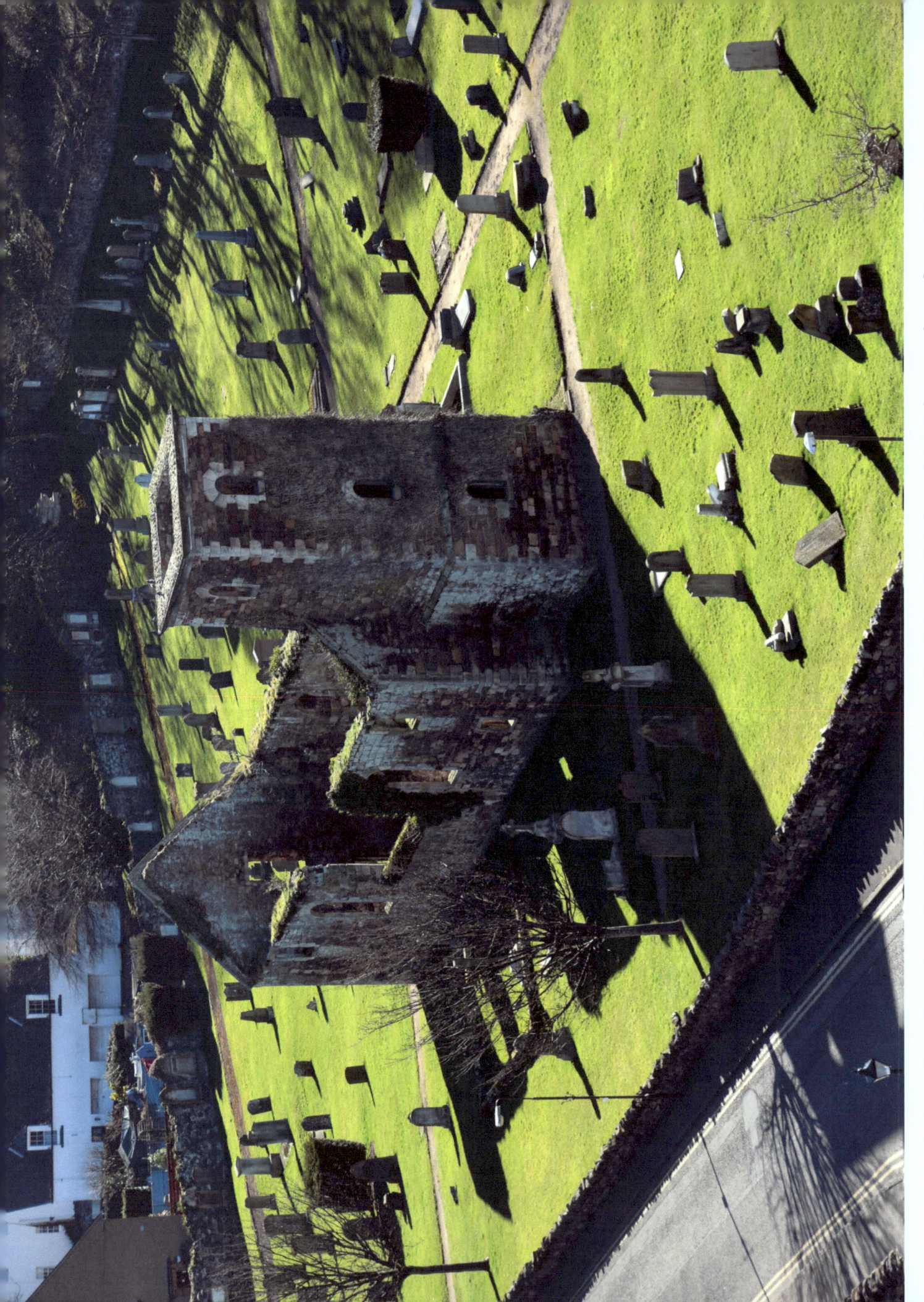

Viewed from St Andrew Blackadder Church tower, St Andrew's Kirk (ruins) in Kirk Ports dates fom 1664

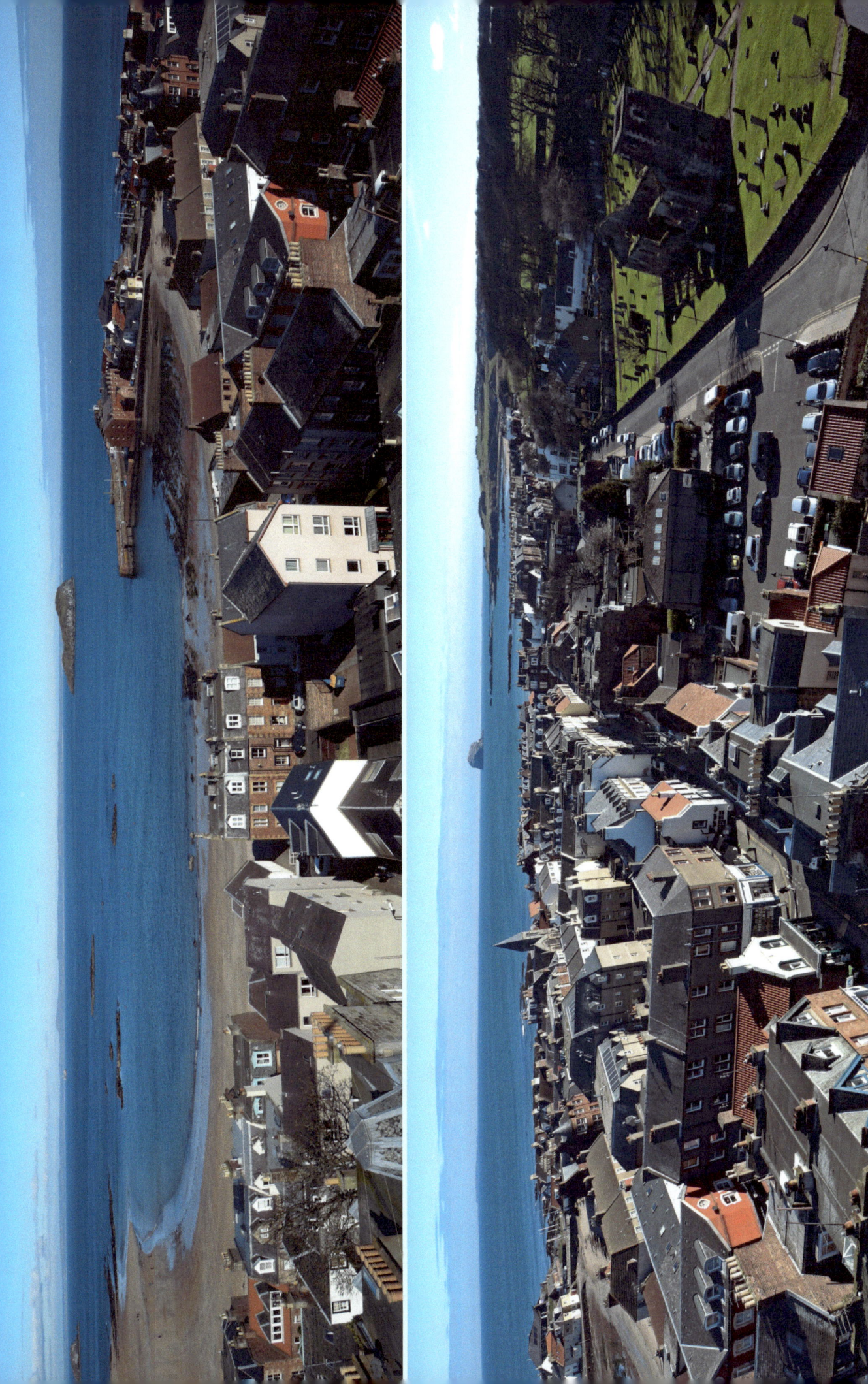

TOP: Looking north from St Andrew Blackadder Church tower
BOTTOM: Looking east from St Andrew Blackadder Church tower

High Street Christmas lights

A snow-covered High Street, looking west from Goodall's Corner

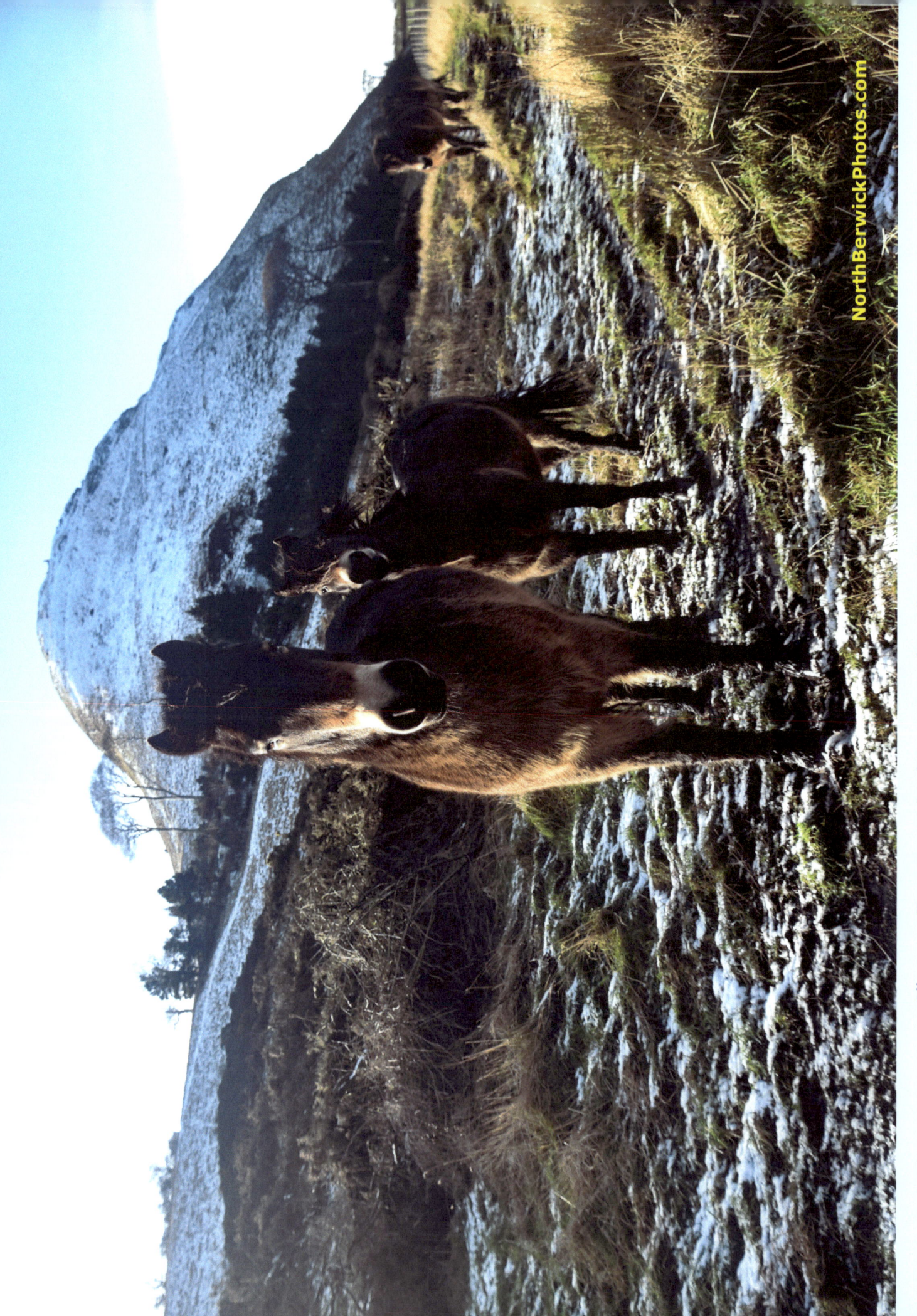

All seven Exmoor ponies have come down from the snow-covered Law

From a microlight, looking east across North Berwick on a bitterly cold and frosty December morning

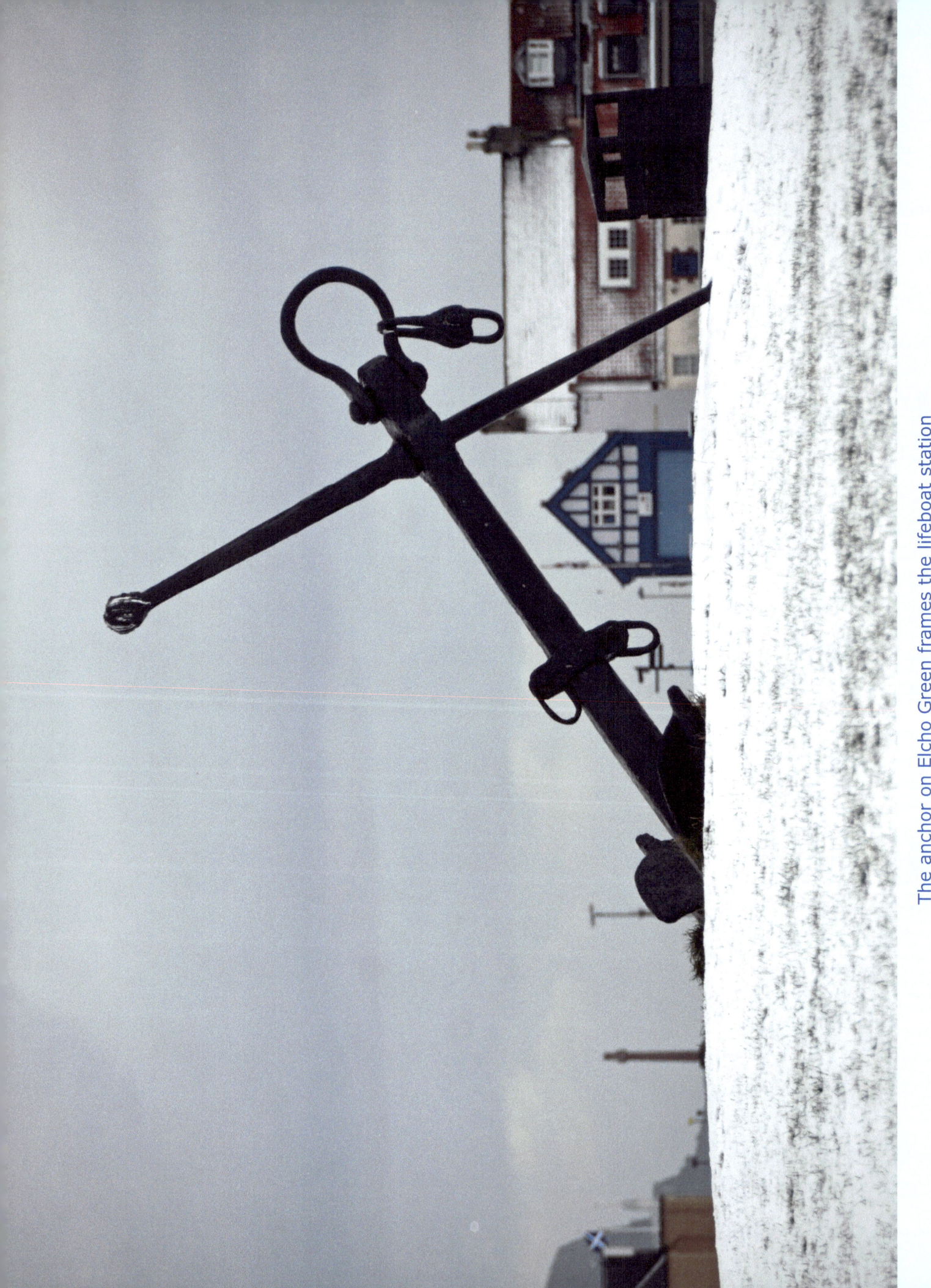

The anchor on Elcho Green frames the lifeboat station

Sledging on East Links putting green (between the tennis courts and the Quadrant)

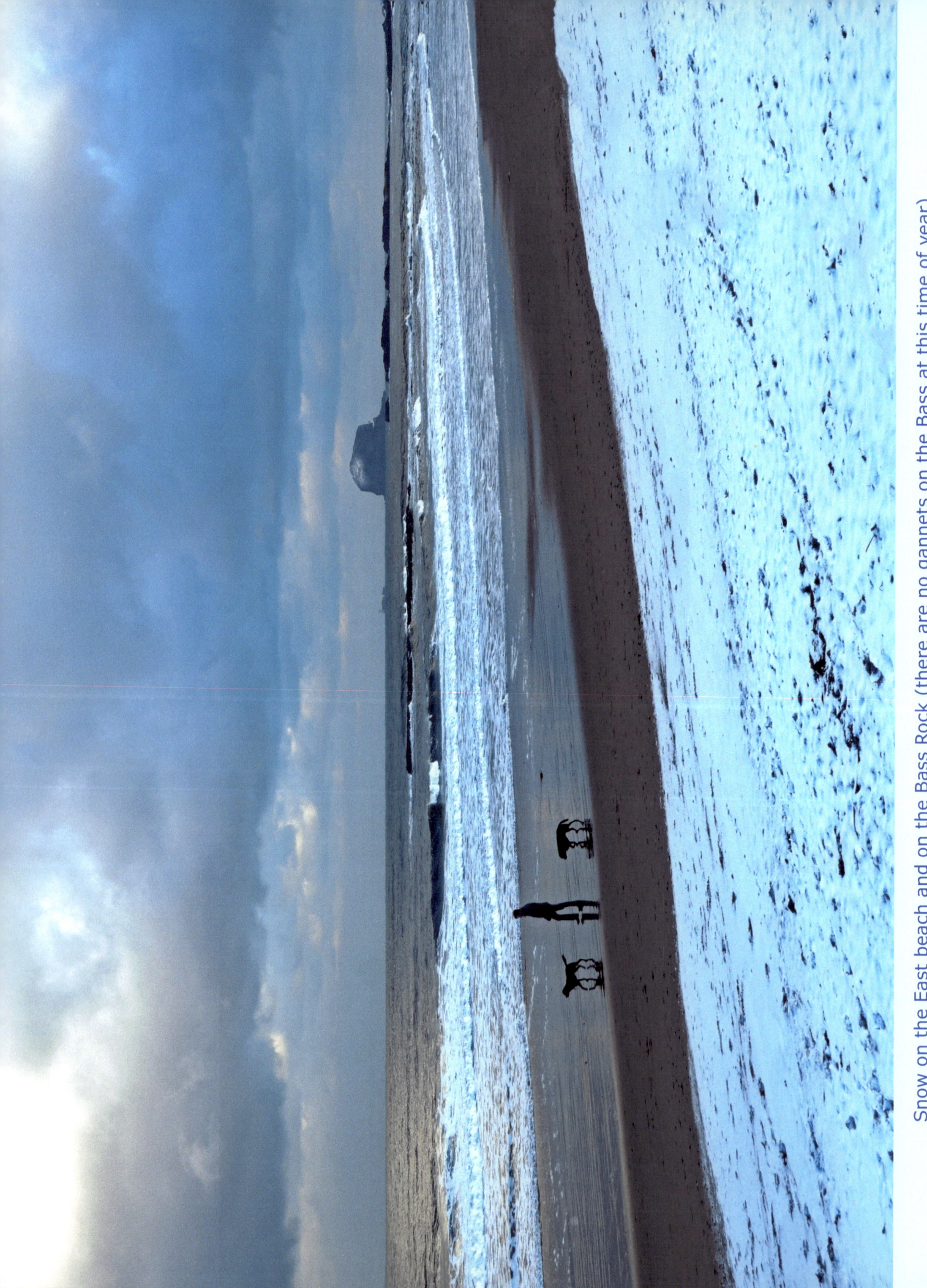

Snow on the East beach and on the Bass Rock (there are no gannets on the Bass at this time of year)

The Boating Pond and East beach

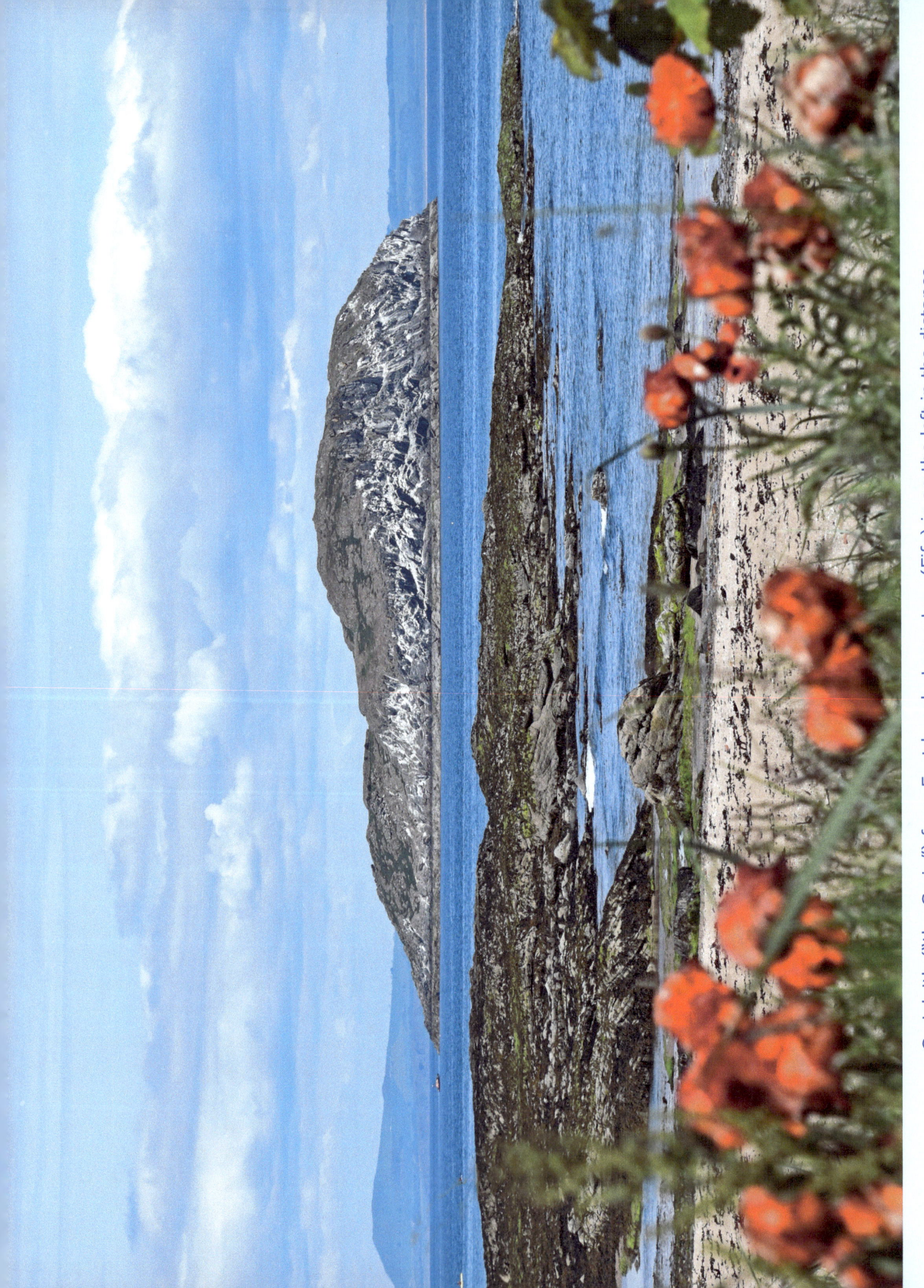

Craigleith ("the Craig") from East beach. Largo Law (Fife) is on the left in the distance

TOP: Milsey Bay and the East beach with the tide out

BOTTOM: Sunset across Milsey Bay. Fidra lighthouse light is flashing

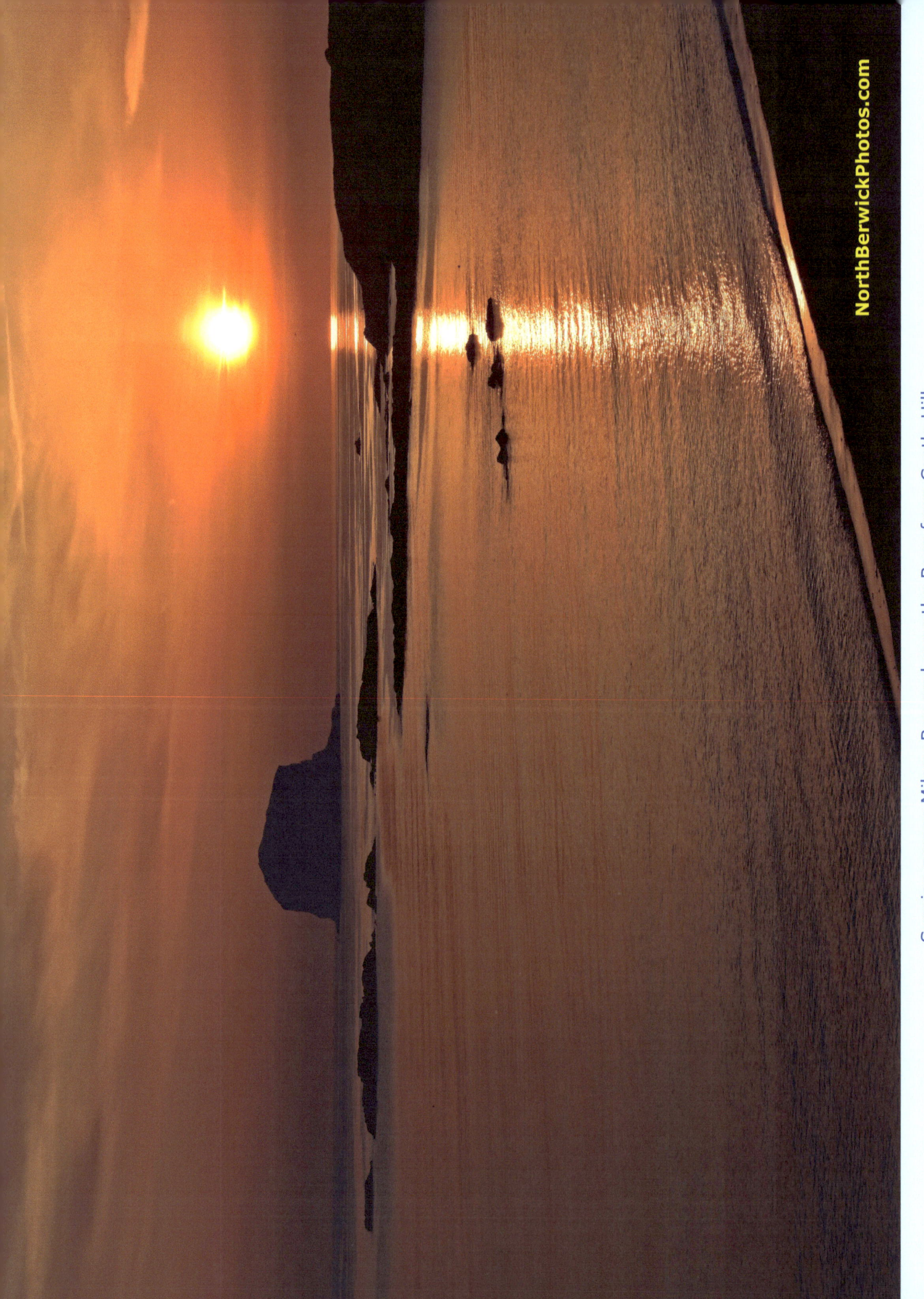

Sunrise across Milsey Bay and over the Bass from Castle Hill

NorthBerwickPhotos.com

Milsey Bay and the Bass Rock

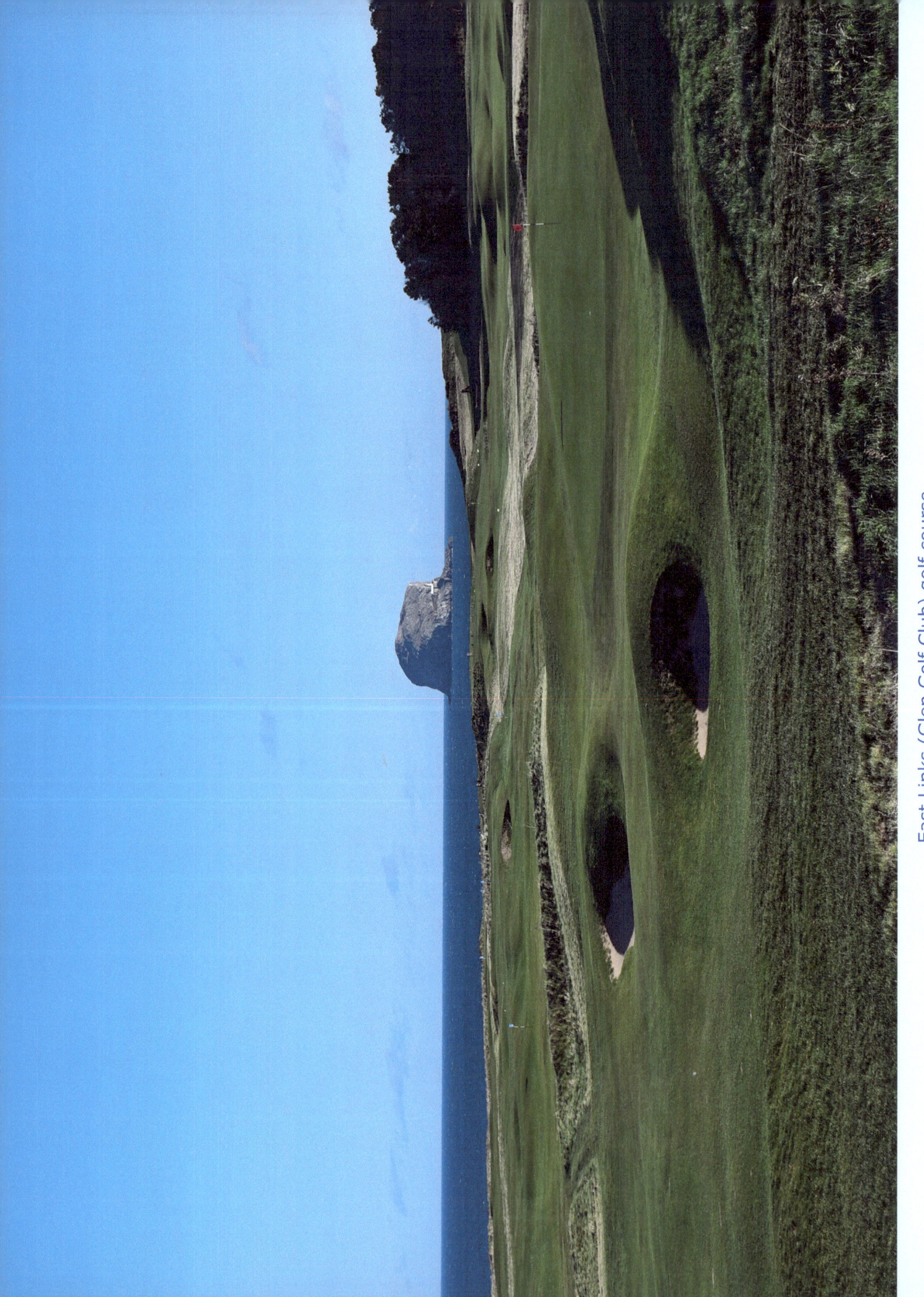

East Links (Glen Golf Club) golf course

Canty Bay, two miles east of North Berwick

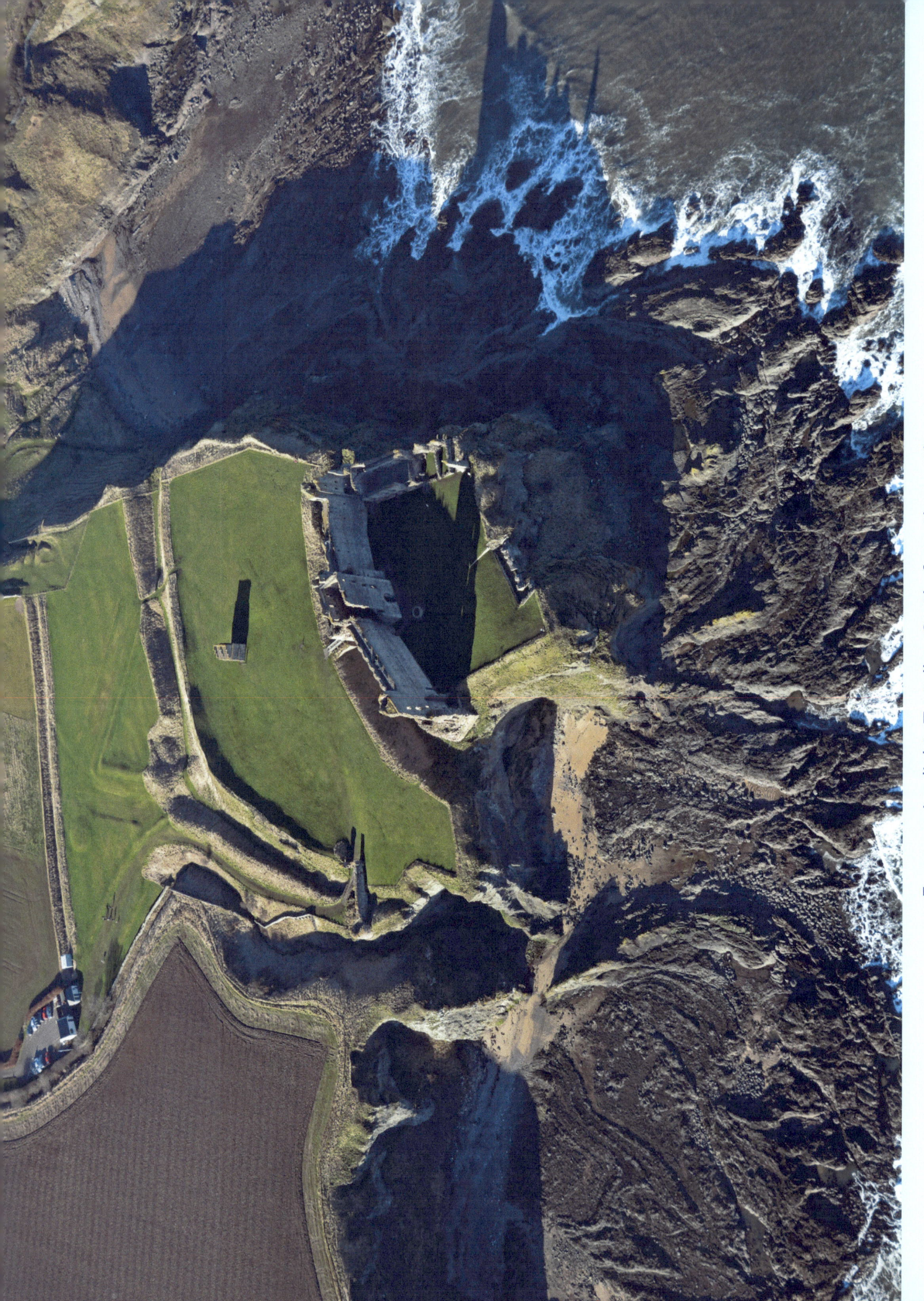

From a microlight, Tantallon Castle from the north

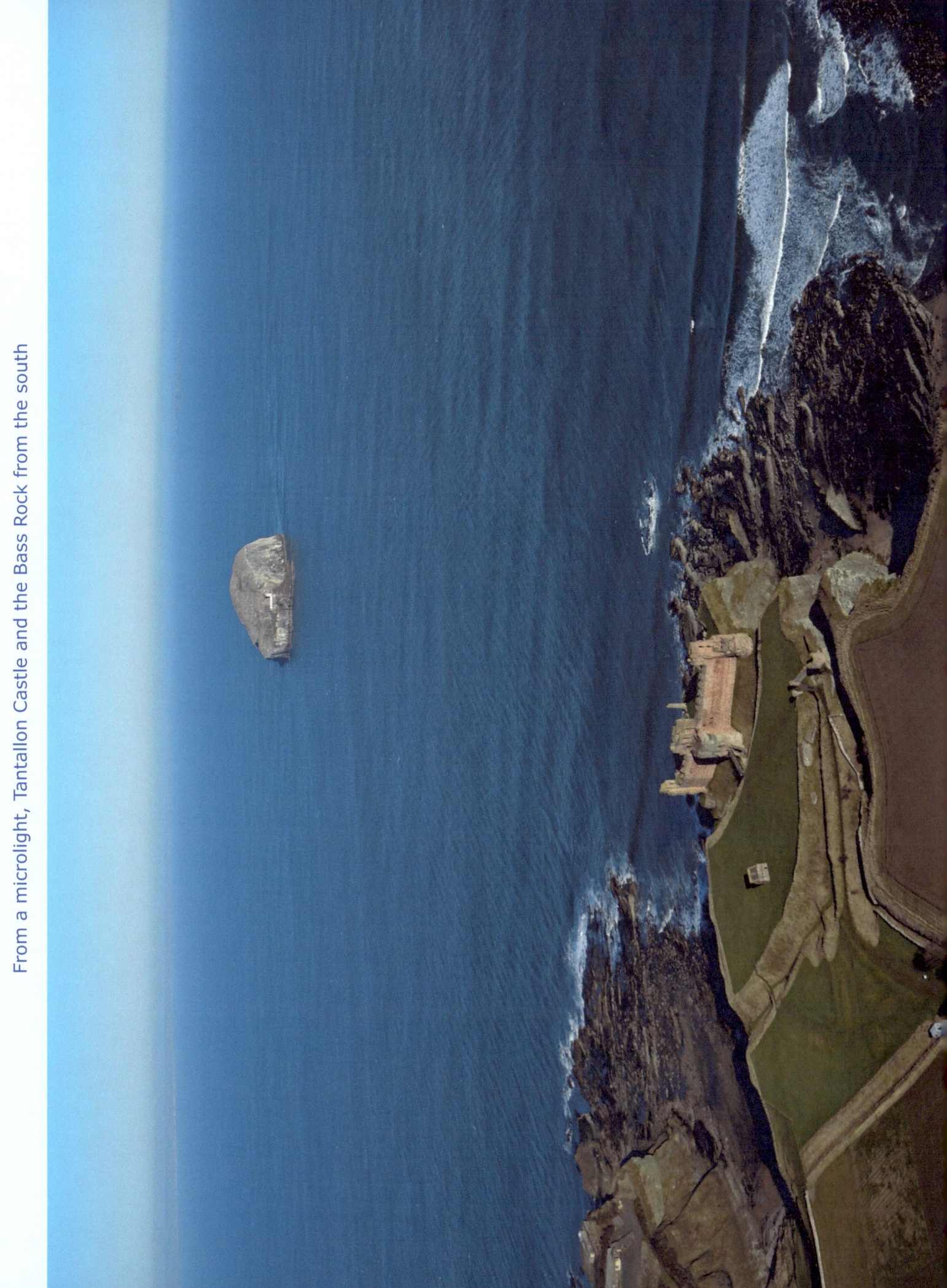

From a microlight, Tantallon Castle and the Bass Rock from the south

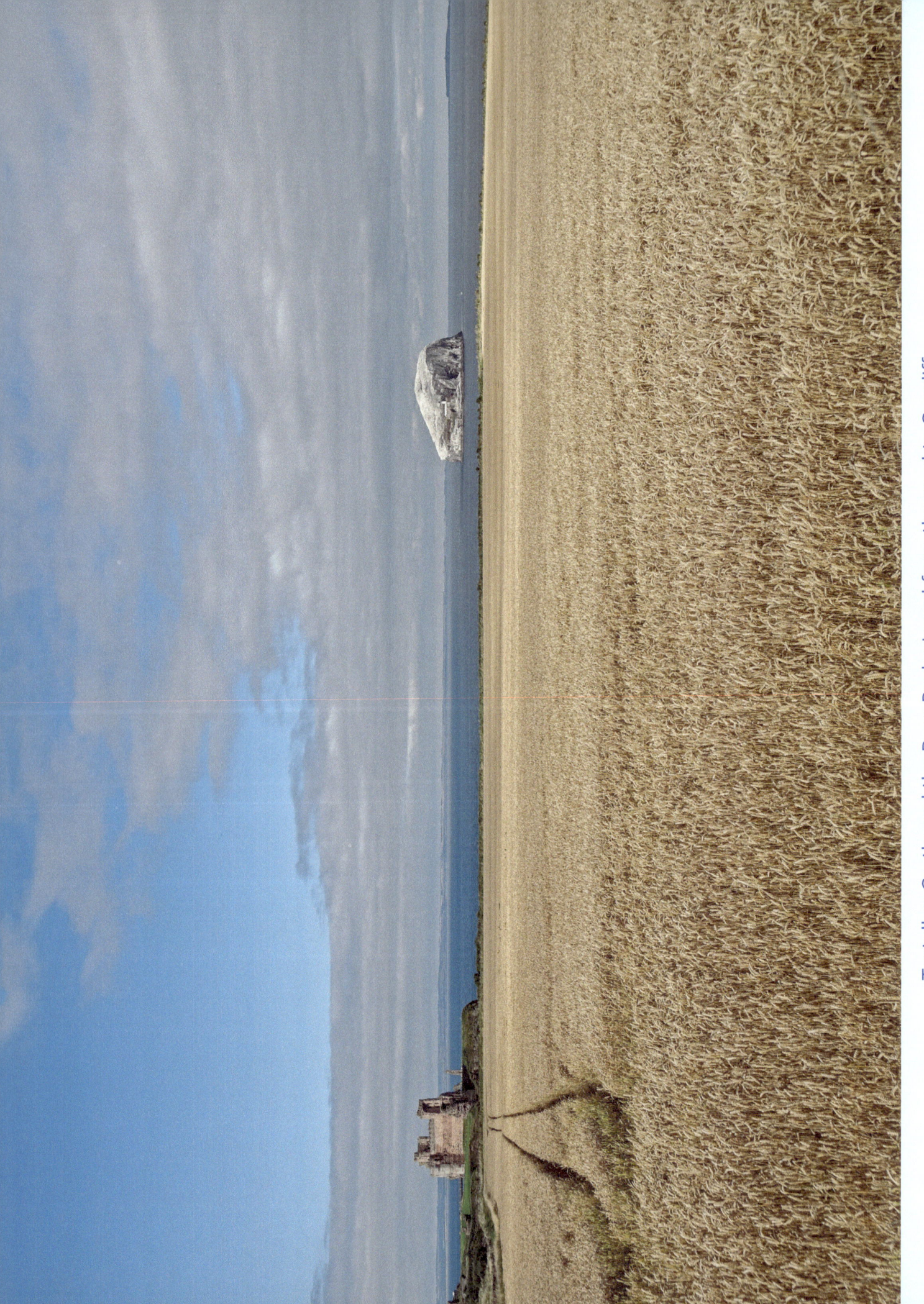

Tantallon Castle and the Bass Rock viewed from the road to Seacliff

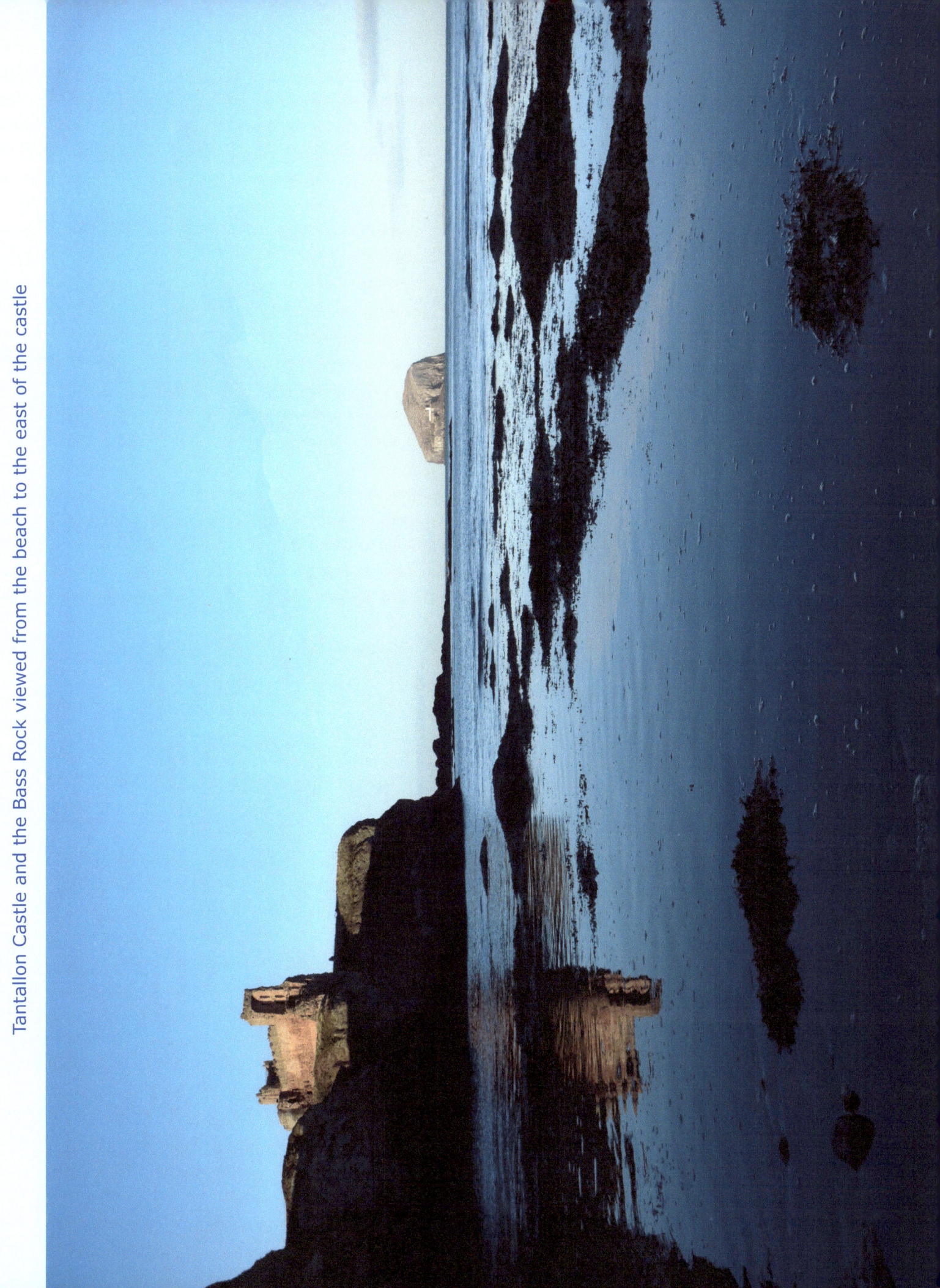

Tantallon Castle and the Bass Rock viewed from the beach to the east of the castle

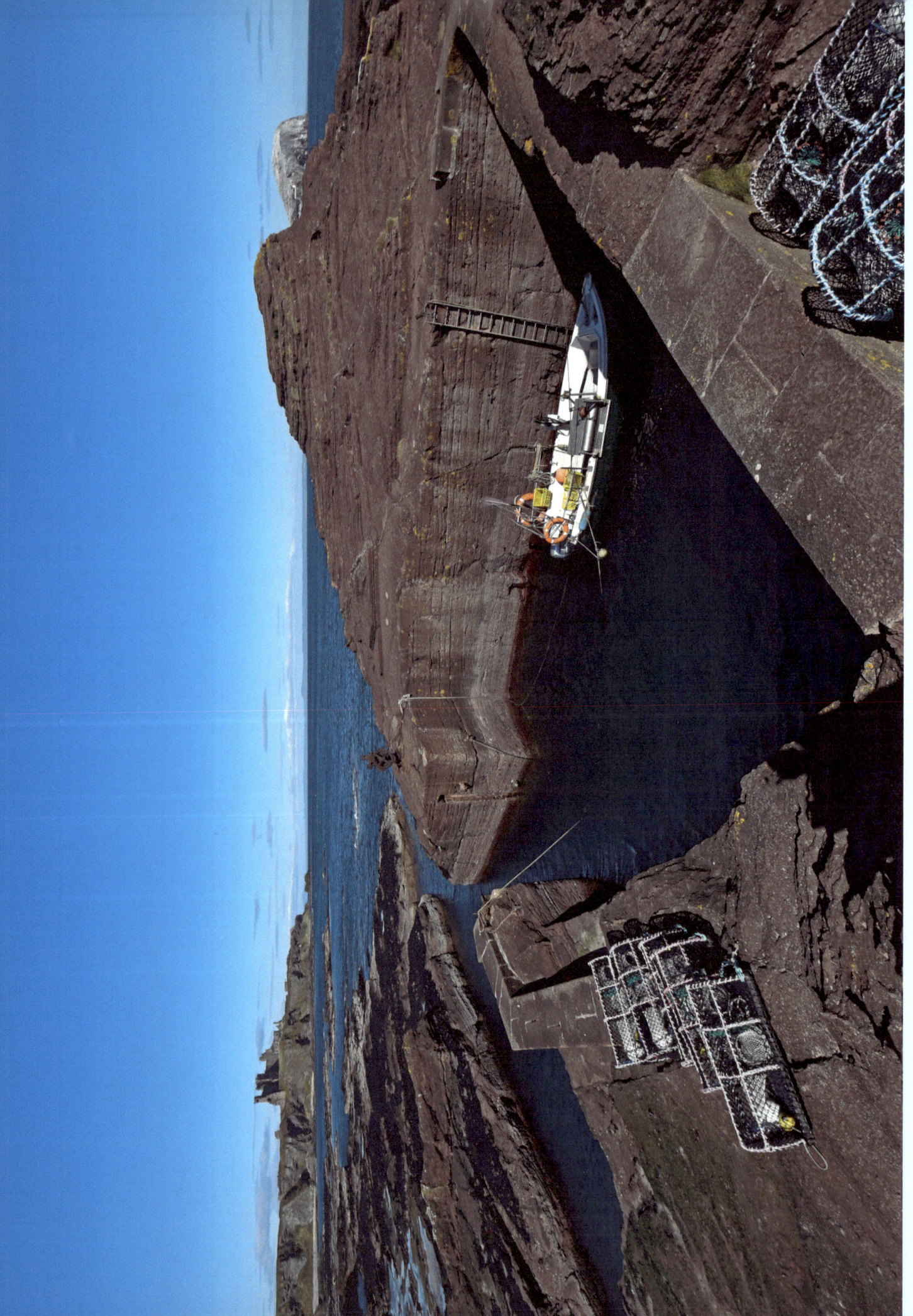

Seacliff harbour with Jack Dale's lobster boat and creels

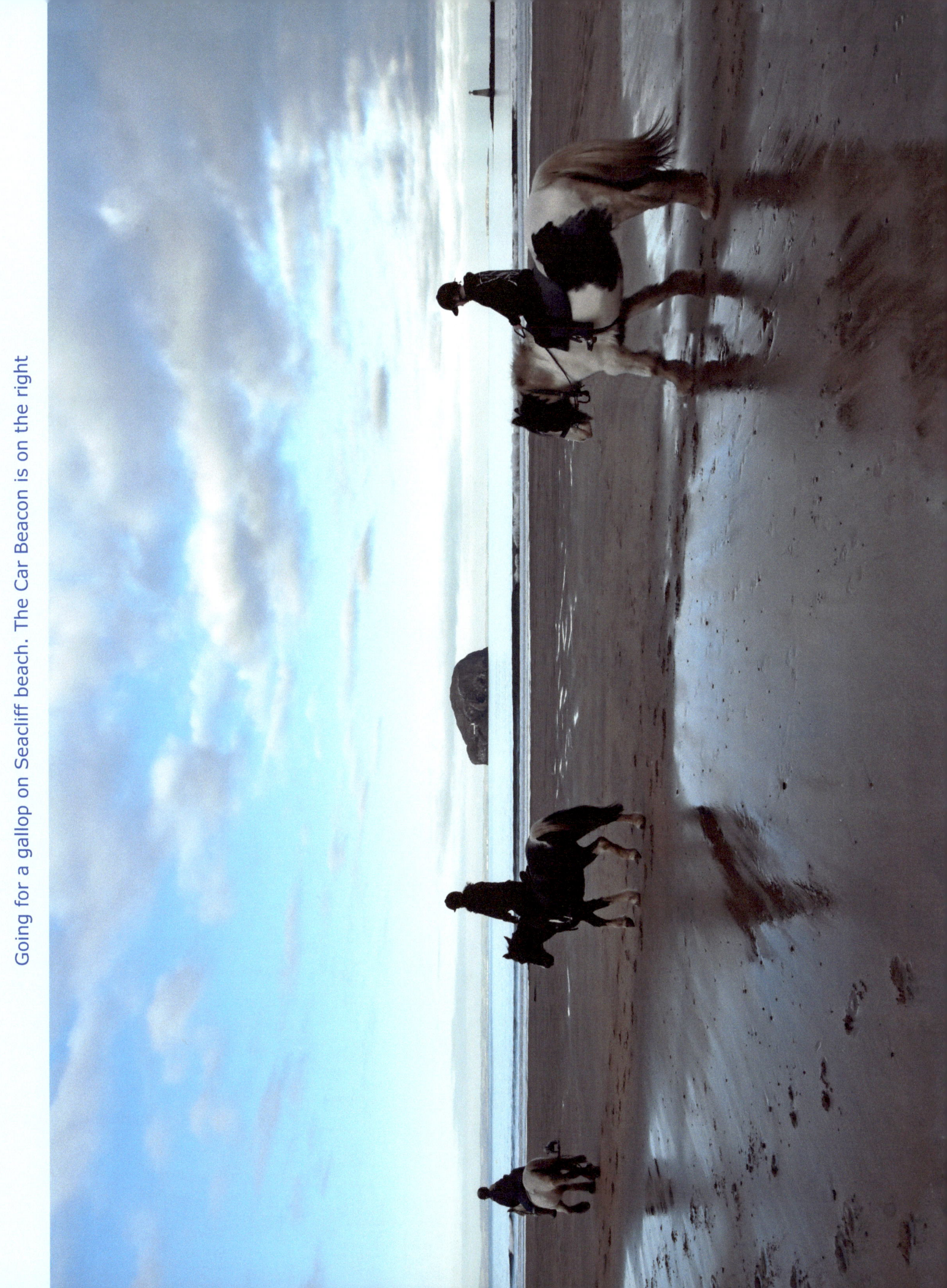

Going for a gallop on Seacliff beach. The Car Beacon is on the right

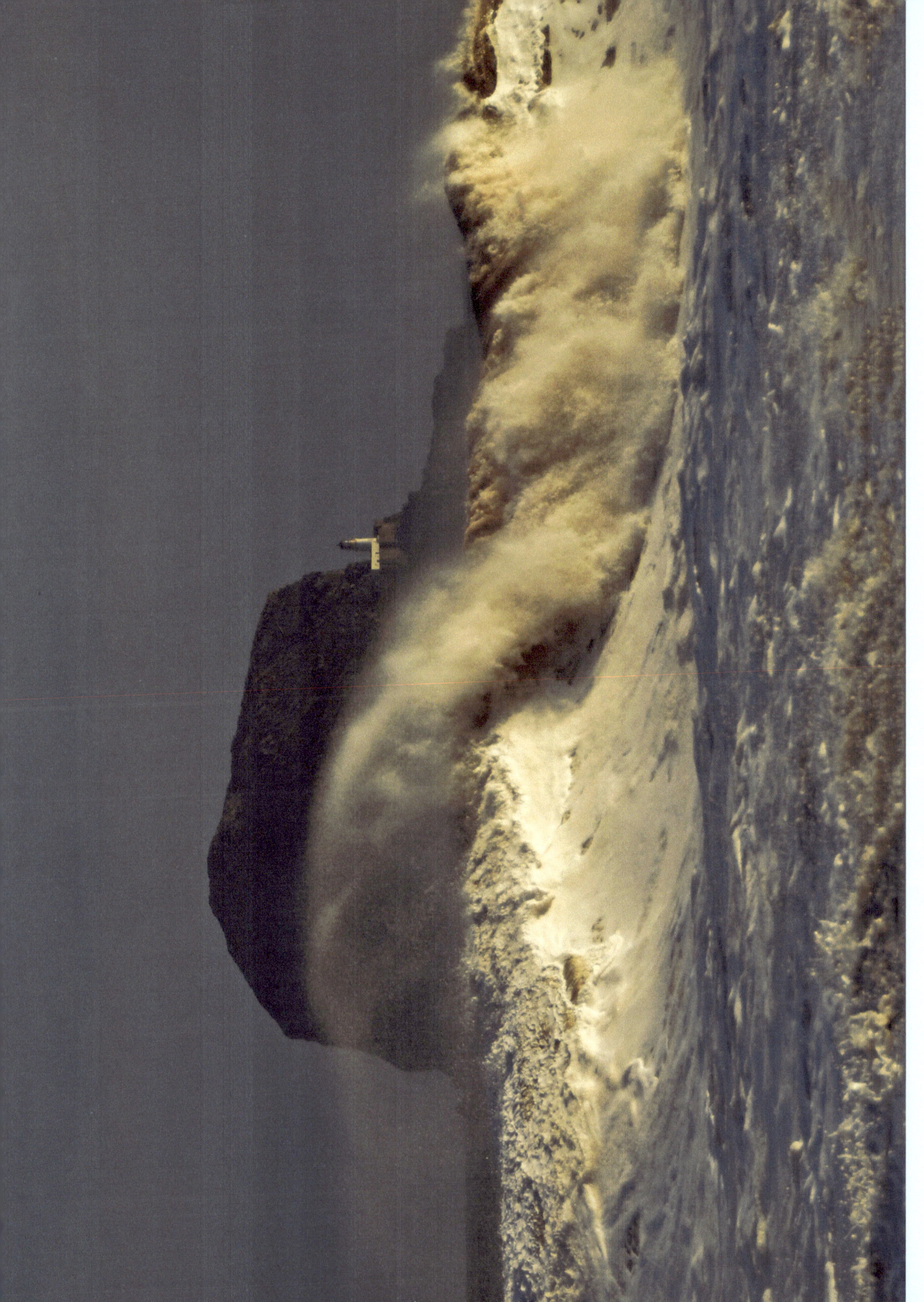

Milsey Bay stormy seas and the Bass Rock

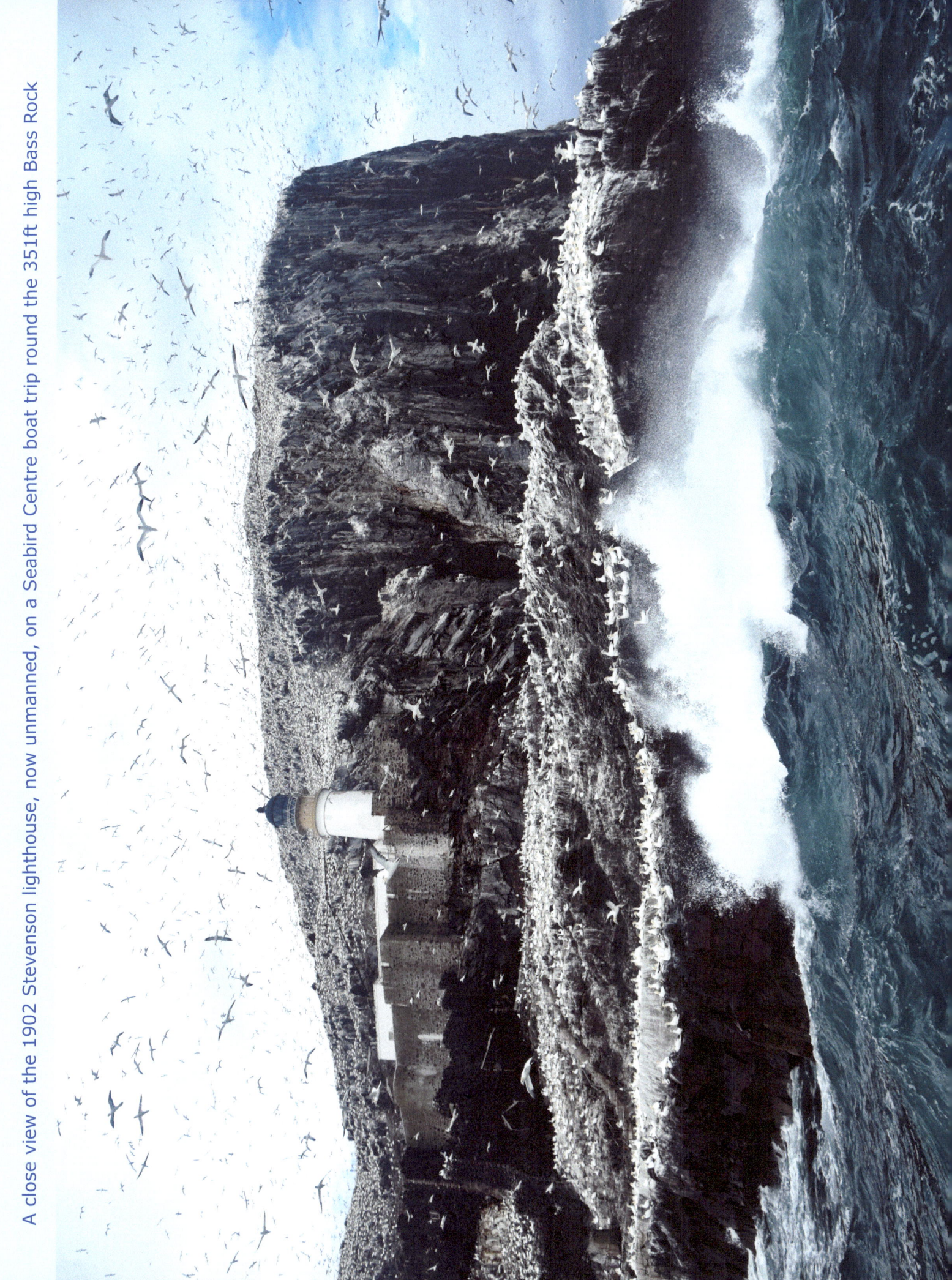

A close view of the 1902 Stevenson lighthouse, now unmanned, on a Seabird Centre boat trip round the 351ft high Bass Rock

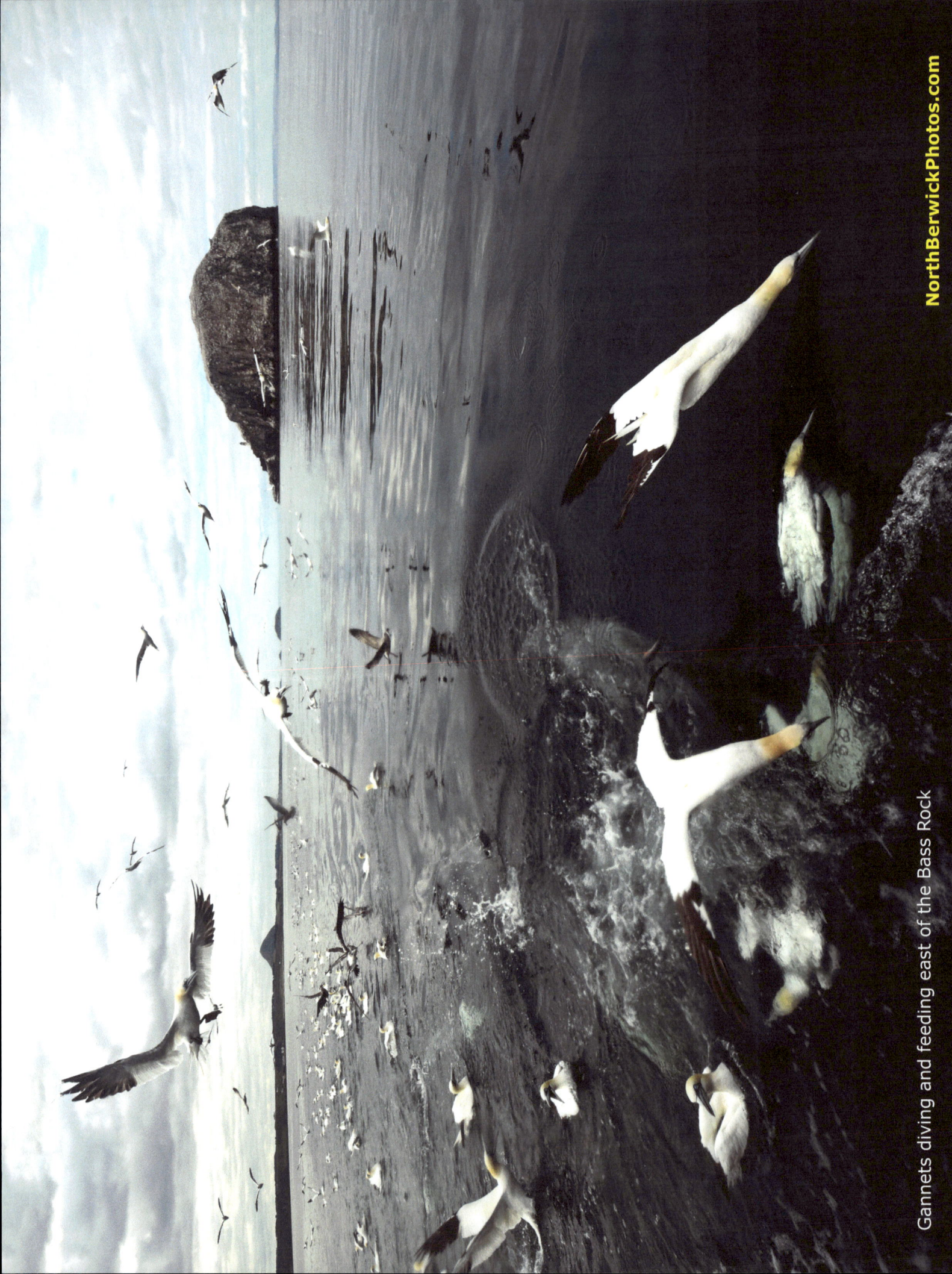

Gannets diving and feeding east of the Bass Rock

NorthBerwickPhotos.com

www.ingramcontent.com/pod-product-compliance
Lightning Source LLC
Chambersburg PA
CBHW040413220526
45473CB00004B/1229